spot

OUTDOOR FUN

BIKING

by Nessa Black

AMICUS | AMICUS INK

helmet

reflector

Look for these
words and pictures
as you read.

bell

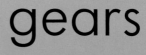

gears

The sun is up. It is a great day for a bike ride. Let's go!

Do you see the helmet?
It keeps the biker's head safe.
Snap! He is ready to roll!

helmet

Do you see the reflector?
It shines when light hits it.

reflector

bell

Do you see the bell?

She rings it. Ring! Ring!

The walkers hear her coming.

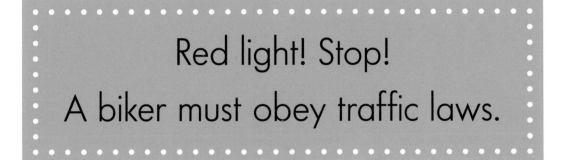

Red light! Stop!
A biker must obey traffic laws.

Do you see the gears?
The biker shifts to a low gear.
Now going up the hill
will be easier.

gears

Look at this bike
for two people.
It is a tandem bike!

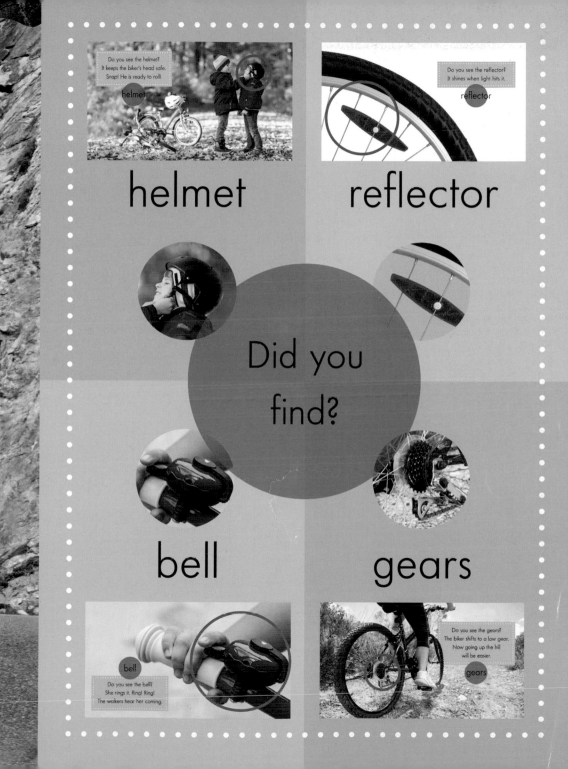

helmet

reflector

Did you find?

bell

gears

sp⊙t

Spot is published by Amicus and Amicus Ink
P.O. Box 1329, Mankato, MN 56002
www.amicuspublishing.us

Wendy Dieker, editor
Deb Miner, series designer
Aubrey Harper, book designer
Shane Freed, photo researcher

Library of Congress Cataloging-in-Publication Data
Names: Black, Nessa, author.
Title: Biking / by Nessa Black.
Description: Mankato, Minnesota : Amicus/Amicus Ink,
[2020] | Series: Spot outdoor fun | Audience: Grade:
K to Grade 3.
Identifiers: LCCN 2019003791 (print) | LCCN 2019014061
(ebook) | ISBN 9781681518473 (pdf) | ISBN
9781681518077 (library binding) | ISBN 9781681525358
(pbk.) | ISBN 9781681518473 (ebk.)
Subjects: LCSH: Cycling--Juvenile literature. | Bicycles--
Juvenile literature. | Picture puzzles--Juvenile literature.
Classification: LCC GV1043.5 (ebook) | LCC GV1043.5
.B56 2020 (print) | DDC 796.6--dc23
LC record available at https://lccn.loc.gov/2019003791

Printed in China

HC   10 9 8 7 6 5 4 3 2 1
PB   10 9 8 7 6 5 4 3 2 1

Photos by VladislavStarozhilov/
iStock cover, 16; DonNichols/iStock
1; monkeybusinessimages/iStock
3; Romrodinka/Dreamstime 4–5;
costasss/iStock 6–7; ra3m/Shutterstock
8–9; Grafissimo/iStock 10–11;
Wavebreakmedia Ltd/Dreamstime 12–
13; H. Mark Weidman Photography/
Alamy 14–15

BIKING